COLOR
and
PRAISE

Published in 2021 by
Harper Design
An Imprint of HarperCollinsPublishers
195 Broadway
New York, NY 10007
Tel: (212) 207-7000
Fax: (855) 746-6023
harperdesign@harpercollins.com
www.hc.com

Distributed throughout North America by
HarperCollinsPublishers
195 Broadway
New York, NY 10007

ISBN 978-0-06-320428-7

Printed in China

First Printing, 2021

Conceived, designed, and produced by
The Bright Press, an imprint of Quarto Publishing plc

Publisher: James Evans
Editorial Director: Isheeta Mustafi
Art Director: Katherine Radcliffe
Managing Editor: Jacqui Sayers
Senior Editor: Caroline Elliker
Design: Studio Noel
Editor: Jerry Pattengale

CREDITS

Unless otherwise stated, all images in this book have been compiled by Studio Noel.
Shutterstock: Alenka Karabanova, Alexkava, Andrii_M, Ann.and.Pen, artpray, AVA
Bitter, Beskova Ekaterina, bessyana, beta757, Christos Georghiou, Daisy and Bumble,
Daria Miazhevich, Dariia Baranova, Digital Bazaar, Dn Br, Erta, eveleen, Extezy,
Gaba Duran, Galina Alex, GoodStudio, HappyPictures, Hein Nouwens, HIGOOD
studio, IvanDbajo, Jorge Ural, Khartseva Tetiana, Liliana Danila, lizanice, Lorelyn
Medina, Magicleaf, Maike Hildebrandt, maljuk, Maor_Winetrob, MicroOne,
molotoka, NTL studio, olegganko, pixelliebe, Proskurina Yuliya, santima.studio,
Shirstok, Simple Line, StockSmartStart, Studio_G, t a k a h i r o, Tartila,
TeddyandMia, TohaHorbenko, Vector Micro Master, vickram, Viktoria Kurpas,
VladisChern, VoodooDot, WarmWorld, world of vector, ya_blue_ko, Yakan.

The Bible verses used within this book have been adapted from the World English
Bible (WEB), which is in the public domain.

COLOR
and
PRAISE

A Biblical Coloring Book for
Rejoicing and Reflection

HARPER
DESIGN

An Imprint of HarperCollinsPublishers

CONTENTS

These select verses represent simple themes—a structure that relates to all of us in our spiritual journeys. We speak, hear, see, feel, and do as we enter our journey of praise. Work through the book from beginning to end, or use the thumbnails below as a visual guide to help you to choose the perfect artwork for your mood.

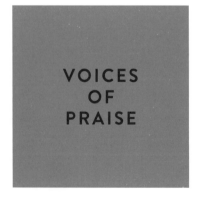

VOICES
OF
PRAISE

1 Chronicles 16:9

18

Psalms 98:1

20

SOUNDS
OF
PRAISE

Psalms 43:4

24

Psalms 30:11–12

26

Ephesians 5:18–20

28

Psalms 147:7

30

Psalms 9:11

32

Psalms 95:1

34

SIGHTS
OF
PRAISE

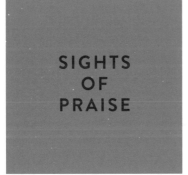

Ephesians 1:3

38

1 Peter 2:9

40

Revelation 5:12

42

Psalms 21:13

44

Psalms 69:34

46

Psalms 116:19

48

Deuteronomy 10:21

50

EXPRESSIONS
OF PRAISE

Psalms 99:9

54

Psalms 100:4

56

Hebrews 13:15–16

58

Isaiah 25:1

60

Mark 14:23

62

Revelation 7:12

64

ACTIONS
OF
PRAISE

2 Samuel 22:4

68

Psalms 35:18

70

Daniel 2:23

72

Psalms 95:6

74

Exodus 15:2

76

PSALMS
118:1

Give thanks to The Lord,
for he is good,
for his loving kindness
endures forever.

Psalms 118:1

78

INTRODUCTION

We all have our favorite moments from our travels. For me, it was standing alone at dusk in the Sistine Chapel. I was staying in the Vatican City facility built by Bob and Dolores Hope, while assisting the Museum of the Bible (DC) with its first Vatican Exhibit (Verbum Domini I). Although it wasn't my first or last time standing in awe of the artists' works, it was indeed the most memorable. I could fully appreciate the height of the paintings and the artistic pinnacle they would establish.

Something else, however, resonated with my soul—the realization that I wasn't in a museum, but a chapel. Regardless of the debate over their cost and personal toll—on Michelangelo especially—or the volumes written on the artists and officials involved, these works have helped millions to worship and praise God for his redemptive story. The artists' illustrative walk through the Bible became an international standard of expression. From the Creation to the Great Judgement, it's all there, including the iconic representation of the moment the finger of God touches that of Adam.

Throughout our recorded history, people have reached out to their god or gods, whether the God of the Bible or some other deity or deities associated with their region or era. We would be hard-pressed not to find spiritual reflections in art and architecture in the history of any group of people. From early Aboriginal art to the gold-plated Buddhist Schwedagon Pagoda in Myanmar, our ancestors have revealed this need to worship and praise a spiritual force. This plays out among millions of artifacts and the stone ruins of religious sites, tens of thousands of extant manuscripts, and an inexhaustible reservoir of printed materials. Christianity's history is no exception. Ancient churches and crosses are found throughout the world, perhaps with the highest artistic expression being found in medieval ruins.

As we collectively learn to live within more pluralistic societies—with many governments trying to foster civil discourse among diverse religious groups—there is an increasing appreciation for a large swath of religious images. Coptic crosses and Catholic chancel screens are as beautiful as a synagogue's Elijah's chair or *Shiviti* (a framed embellishment of Psalms 16:8). And we could continue through most religions; whether the great Egyptian pyramids or the Parthenon Sculptures (Elgin Marbles) reflecting the mythological Greek pantheon, we gaze in awe. Perhaps the best displays of representative respect for religious architecture and beauty are two buildings with a shared Islamic and Christian history, but in reverse order. The magnificent Church of Hagia Sophia of Constantinople was repurposed as a mosque, then a UNESCO World Heritage Site, then back to a mosque in 2020 (though still open to tourists). Conversely, the Great Mosque of Córdoba is now the Great Mosque-Cathedral of Córdoba, or officially today the Cathedral of Our Lady of the Assumption.

My work has taken me to hundreds of inspiring chapels and cathedrals, often entering to the sounds of a Gregorian chant, or a tourist serendipitously singing to hear the majestic echoes. Sanctuaries were created to praise God, and artisans were tasked with treating even the most hard-to-reach spaces with special attention. Perhaps you're on a similar journey with this book. Regardless of who sees it, you have an express purpose in spending time illuminating it. And who knows, maybe centuries from now someone in your family line might rediscover your commitment to beauty, and your expressive hues of praise.

JERRY PATTENGALE, PhD

University professor, Indiana Wesleyan University
Senior Advisor to the President, Museum of the Bible, DC.
Author of *Inexplicable: How Christianity Spread to the Ends of the Earth* with corresponding TV series, and *The New Book of Christian Martyrs* (Tyndale House).

PRAISE THROUGH COLORING

In this book we focus on one religion—Christianity. Throughout its Old Testament (or the Hebrew Bible of Judaism) and New Testament, we find ample expressions of praise.

However fast your mind might be moving, keep in mind that the gorgeous thirteenth-century Chartres Cathedral took almost thirty years to build and required a team of around 300 artisans. The effort was to help God's people to pause and praise, not unlike the journey before you.

The beautifully illustrated verses within this book have been carefully selected for their uplifting nature. Take a moment to read a passage, then reflect on the verse as you allow the simple act of coloring to relax and focus your mind on the act of praise. This process is a wonderful and creative way to strengthen your connection to God and to the Church.

MATERIALS

A small pack of twelve colored pencils or felt-tip pens is all you need to enjoy this book. Pencils will need to be kept sharp for maximum control in the detailed areas.

Some sections of the page are printed with foil to help re-create the effect of illumination. The foil can't be colored over, but you can choose colors that will complement these as well as experiment with metallic pens of your own.

Voices of
PRAISE

PSALMS

28:7

The Lord is my strength and my shield.
My heart has trusted in him, and I am helped.
Therefore my heart greatly rejoices.
With my song I will thank him.

PSALMS

34:1

I will bless the Lord at all times.
His praise will always be in my mouth.

P SALMS
119:171

Let my lips utter praise,
for you teach me your statutes.

1 CHRONICLES

16:9

Sing to him.
Sing praises to him.
Tell of all his marvelous works.

PSALMS

98:1

Sing to the Lord a new song,
for he has done marvelous things!
His right hand and his holy arm have
worked salvation for him.

Sounds of
PRAISE

Psalms

43:4

Then I will go to the altar of God,
to God, my exceeding joy.
I will praise you on the harp, God, my God.

PSALMS
30:11–12

You have turned my mourning into dancing
for me. You have removed my sackcloth,
and clothed me with gladness,
to the end that my heart may sing
praise to you, and not be silent. Lord my
God, I will give thanks to you forever!

EPHESIANS

5:18–20

Don't be drunken with wine, in which is
dissipation, but be filled with the Spirit,
speaking to one another in psalms, hymns,
and spiritual songs; singing and making
melody in your heart to the Lord;
giving thanks always concerning all things
in the name of our Lord Jesus Christ,
to God, even the Father.

Psalms

147:7

Sing to the Lord with thanksgiving.
Sing praises on the harp to our God.

Psalms
9:11

Sing praises to the Lord, who dwells in Zion,
and declare among the people what he has done.

PSALMS
95:1

Oh come, let's sing to the Lord.
Let's shout aloud to the rock of our salvation!

Sights of
PRAISE

Ephesians
1:3

Blessed be the God and Father of our
Lord Jesus Christ, who has blessed us with
every spiritual blessing in the heavenly
places in Christ.

1 PETER

2:9

But you are a chosen race, a royal priesthood,
a holy nation, a people for God's own
possession, that you may proclaim the
excellence of him who called you out of
darkness into his marvelous light.

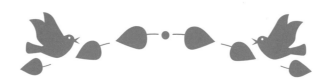

REVELATION

5:12

Saying with a loud voice, "Worthy is the Lamb who has been killed to receive the power, wealth, wisdom, strength, honor, glory, and blessing!"

PSALMS
21:13

Be exalted, Lord, in your strength,
so we will sing and praise your power.

Psalms
69:34

Let heaven and earth praise him;
the seas, and everything that moves therein!

PSALMS
116:19

In the courts of the Lord's house,
In the middle of you, Jerusalem.
Praise the Lord!

DEUTERONOMY

10:21

He is your praise, and he is your God,
who has done for you these great and
awesome things which your eyes have seen.

Expressions of
PRAISE

PSALMS
99:9

Exalt the Lord, our God.
Worship at his holy hill,
for the Lord, our God, is holy!

PSALMS

100:4

Enter into his gates with thanksgiving,
and into his courts with praise.
Give thanks to him, and bless his name.

HEBREWS

13:15–16

Through him, then, let's offer up
a sacrifice of praise to God continually,
that is, the fruit of lips which
proclaim allegiance to his name.
But don't forget to be doing good and
sharing, for with such sacrifices
God is well pleased.

ISAIAH

25:1

Lord, you are my God. I will exalt you! I will praise your name, for you have done wonderful things, things planned long ago, in complete faithfulness and truth.

MARK

14:23

He took the cup, and when he had given
thanks, he gave to them. They all drank of it.

REVELATION
7:12

"Amen! Blessing, glory, wisdom,
thanksgiving, honor, power, and might,
be to our God forever and ever! Amen."

Actions of
PRAISE

2 SAMUEL

22:4

I call on the Lord, who is worthy to be praised;
So shall I be saved from my enemies.

PSALMS
35:18

I will give you thanks in the great assembly.
I will praise you among many people.

Daniel

2:23

I thank you and praise you,
O God of my fathers,
who have given me wisdom and might,
and have now made known to me
what we desired of you;
for you have made known to
us the king's matter.

PSALMS
95:6

Oh come, let's worship and bow down.
Let's kneel before the Lord, our Maker.

EXODUS

15:2

The Lord is my strength and song.
He has become my salvation.
This is my God, and I will praise Him;
my father's God, and I will exalt Him.

PSALMS
118:1

Give thanks to the Lord,
for he is good,
for his loving kindness
endures forever.